FullStack SalesPerson
A Guide to Selling in Today's Hi-Tech World

Archan Bahulekar

Robin Lee

CONTENTS

ACKNOWLEDGMENTS

In the writing of this book, I have many people whom I would like to thank. First and foremost are my wife Moira, my daughter Christina, and my soon-to-be-born son Andrew. Family is everything to me, and their support is life-affirming and means the world to me.

I would especially like to thank the late Prof. Steve Corio, who taught my Sales Management class at Santa Clara University. Steve was a huge influence in my career as well as a mentor and friend. Rest in peace and thank you for all the valuable lessons you have taught me.

I have also been inspired by many salespersons over the years: CB Lee, Jolyn Lee, Bernard King, Paris Alexi, Ben Greenberg, Carl Guichard, David Showumni, Abdi Warsame, Prem Singh, Nicholas Bernie, Alwyn Evans, Smiley Wang, Hadleigh Rossiter, Matt Curtis, Stuart Bingham, Joe Schwartz, Ted McKinney, Steve Chan, Kristina Klein Festa, Genelle Hung, Scott Barneson, Larry Mintz, Stanley Chia, Edwin Lim, Pauline Chan, Adrian Pay, Steve Tunstall, and Mark Pickard. Without them, this book would not exist.

Finally, I would like to thank Archan Bahulekar, my co-author and one of the best salespersons I know. We've embarked on various successful initiatives together, and those experiences combined with his determination to complete this book, in which he played a leading role, are a testament to his drive, resilience and grit. Onward and upward, my friend!

Robin Lee

I dedicate this book to my mother Anjali Bahulekar, my wife Supriya and other major influences in my life – late Mrs Meena*tai* Tirodkar, late Mr Prabhakar Bhide, late Mrs Shakuntala Sathaye and late Mrs Adelaide Alphonso. Thanks to them, I graduated from writing meaningless poems to short articles in news dailies to eventually writing a book.

The very basics and foundations in consultative selling of hi-tech solutions were introduced to me at an early age by my father, Milind Bahulekar. Over the years, I've had the good fortune of learning the true meaning of being a FullStack Salesperson from experienced and awe-inspiring professionals like Ruston Townson, Luis Carrillo, Jon Hanmer, Suyin Lee, Naoto Matsushita, Frank Nguyen, Antione Lamy and Vishal Nagpal.

A special thanks to my co-author Robin Lee for embarking on this project. Your high-octane energy is contagious and a source of constant inspiration in the pursuit of professional and personal excellence.

Robin and I would like to thank Ashwin Dutt for the cover design and Blackwater Communications for providing editorial and publishing support.

Archan Bahulekar

FOREWORD

'Sell me this pen.'

Every salesperson has surely heard this question, whether during an interview or simply as a challenge from a non-sales friend. There are many *typical* ways to respond: *'This is the best pen in the market'*, *'This is a very smooth pen'*, or *'This is a classy pen'*. One could argue that all of these are *poor* ways of trying to sell a pen, as they ignore a most *fundamental* question:

'What do you need this pen for, and what value do you intend to derive from it?'

Salespersons of old would probably just start talking, without spending much time on such questions, and push the product on you. Therefore, they may have been considered aggressive, flashy, or dishonest or as having an attitude or a hidden agenda. Because of these qualities, people (perhaps, even salespersons) may have a negative impression of sales. Some might not even consider salespersons to be *professionals*.

To the salesperson (newbie or veteran) reading this book, fear not, because a professional is exactly what you are. *Today's salespersons* play multiple roles—business stakeholder, client's problem solver, and liaison between company and client. Quite simply, they do a lot more than *yesterday's salespersons* in the dynamic environment they operate in.

This book is aimed at enabling you, the *salesperson of today*, to become the *FullStack salesperson of tomorrow*, that is, the person who owns the sales process from start to finish and beyond. The processes, techniques, and best practices contained herein should guide you to make this step up and thus drive both your company and your clients to greater success.

WHAT IS 'SALES'?

Is Sales an Art or a Science?

Selling involves the ability to influence people to buy something that they might not even realize they want or need. This calls for some dramatic flair and a winning personality on the salesperson's part. Does this mean that sales is an *art*?

At the same time, studies in the field of *social psychology* have looked at how people are influenced by one another. Furthermore, studies in the field of *communication theory* have provided significant insights into how people can be influenced. Then, does this mean that sales is a *science*?

If you ask these questions to sales trainers, they would argue that selling is *both*: an art and a science. Salespersons who focus only on the *art* of selling will not be able to scale or sustain their results. At the same time, salespersons who treat selling as only a *science* will lose out on businesses and clients who value relationships as the cornerstone of selling.

Research has demonstrated that how a person perceives and interprets a message is influenced by how the message is conveyed. If information alone could result in a positive buying decision, salespersons would be unnecessary. However, surveys of people's buying behaviours have revealed that a buy decision is often based not on the features, quality, or even price of a product or service but on the salesperson. Harvard Business School Professors Benson P. Shapiro and John J. Sviokla noted that *'Despite the tremendous contributions of information and communications technology, selling is still largely a function of interpersonal relations, which are guided by the artful ability to recognize motivations, needs, and perceptions'*. Therefore, the ability to influence a prospective buyer is a survival skill rather than a luxury for a salesperson.

Previously, the specific factors that influenced people remained a mystery. The actual process of influence had never been broken down, analysed, and studied, and therefore, it was mainly considered an art. However, many studies have now focused on understanding exactly what creates and enables influence. Behaviours and mindsets that support and enhance influence have been studied in detail, and the results have revolutionized the understanding of how influence is actually produced. Researchers have now applied rigorous scientific approaches to identify and understand which messages lead people to accept, surrender, or change. Furthermore, they have used systematic processes to replicate successful results, thus proving that selling is also a science.

Communication theory shows how verbal and nonverbal communication heighten or reduce the persuasiveness of an appeal. This is why social psychologists say that people can improve their ability to influence others by learning and implementing persuasion strategies that have proved successful in the past. Irrespective of recent developments in fields such as artificial intelligence and technology, one cannot ignore the art of selling. More than B2B (business-to-business) or even B2C (business-to-consumer), sales will always be *P2P*, that is, people to people. Therefore, to be successful, salespersons must use the science of selling to *guide* the art of selling and then leverage best practices to deliver results.

What are the Main Objectives of Sales?

Put simply, the main objective of sales is to attract more customers, sell more goods, and be more profitable than the competition. However, this is easier said than done. Setting up sales strategies and objectives is a much more complex process. Your decision-making should be guided by the sales objectives and goals listed below.

Bring new customers onboard: Obviously, you can only make a sale when you have a customer to sell to. Therefore, you will need to make efforts to reach out to potential customers and convince them that your product/service is what they need, so that they will buy from you. Also, once you have got these customers onboard, remember to hold on to them, as repeat customers will likely account for the major proportion of your sales in the long run.

Bring in revenue: Sales is the only business function that generates revenue. Your company makes money when it sells products/services. The resulting revenue is what keeps the company running, including paying for your salary!

Make profits: The main objective of any business is to make profits, whether large or small (but preferably large!). In simple terms, *profit = revenue − cost*. As noted above, making sales is what generates revenue, and the more sales you make, the higher will be your revenue. Then, focus on keeping your costs low to increase your profit. Often, you will find that it is those big deals you dream of clinching that will keep your company's profits healthy.

Improve sales efficiency: Studies have shown that having an effective sales strategy and knowing the right things to do are what differentiate a top salesperson from an average one. You must carefully examine sales processes to improve sales efficiency. In doing so, sales analytics; key performance indicators (KPIs); and metrics such as call rates, sales cycle lengths, and lead conversion rates can be used to identify what works and what does not. You can create dashboards to visualize trends and plan future strategies and even use customer relationship management (CRM) and sales enablement tools (e.g., *Seismic*) to align sales processes and goals and improve sales efficiency.

Generate more leads and improve lead quality: An ideal lead possesses certain key attributes that influences their likelihood to buy your product/service. These attributes include annual sales, employee count, industry vertical, job title, and current use of a competitor's service or product. When a prospective client searches for your product/service online, it helps if you have used search engine optimization (SEO) to ensure that you appear on the first page of the search engine results. In the case of B2B sales, advertising or being part of an association of companies, business federation, or chamber of commerce can help generate sales leads. If you develop a strong relationship with your existing clients, they could prove to be a great source of more sales leads.

Scope the market: To be a top salesperson, you must be willing to boldly go where no one has gone before. In other words, try new avenues and angles to reach and convince your customer, analyse the market using different approaches or even metrics to gain new insights, and learn what the competitors are doing so that you can outsmart them.

Develop products and innovate: Customer feedback can help you identify areas that work well as well as areas that need improvement in your product/service. Use this feedback to develop and improve them, as it will give your company a better offering and make things better for existing and future customers. Similarly, customer feedback can also give you new ideas. For example, if customers request features that you do not currently offer, it could help you innovate and develop improved or even new products/services. In this way, you can help your company adapt and grow in response to changing market demands.

While identifying strategic sales objectives for yourself, ensure that you go beyond superficial issues like how many products to order or when to conduct special promotions and sales. If you successfully create a complete buying experience for your customer by aligning the entire product development process, you can increase the chances of your customer coming back for more. You must have an awareness of your strengths and weaknesses and match these to market opportunities to ensure that what you are offering is what the customer will want.

Do We Need Sales?

Above, we have looked at sales and its purpose from the viewpoint of the salesperson. But what about the customer's viewpoint? Customers have traditionally thought of salespersons as pushy people who shove unnecessary products down their throat, so their first instinct is to run away from them. Also, if you are a customer with a smartphone and therefore have easy access to information, why would you need a salesperson?

So, if technology makes the salesperson redundant, do we even need sales? The answer to this question lies in basic human nature. Everyone wants to make a *safe buy decision*. We need an informed and educated voice telling us about the pros and cons of buying a product. Therefore, in today's environment, salespersons must reinvent themselves to be guides instead of being the aggressive sellers of old.

One way of achieving this is to combine automation

with human ingenuity. For example, if a visitor on your website has shown interest in a product or asked for a price list, thoroughly research their needs, choose the right time for a conversation, and call them to discuss their problems and possible solutions. The ability to be action-oriented and forward-thinking will differentiate a top salesperson from an average one. Because a customer will not want to make an unwise decision, you can guide them toward the right decision by using all the relevant information you have researched beforehand and thus win their trust.

To close a deal and grow aggressively, your prospective customer must enjoy an amazing experience from the first time they look at your website or talk to you to when they become actual customers. You will be primarily responsible for delivering this amazing experience. Then, the next challenge before you will be to scale the successful processes that helped deliver this experience and to repeat them to deliver the same results for the next customer.

To be an effective salesperson, you need to be armed with processes, practices, technologies, and tools to improve performance and productivity. Even today, a combination of marketing technology and an informed salesperson remains the best bet for converting leads to customers.

A BRIEF HISTORY OF SALES

Sales and the Industrial Revolution

Selling is considered the world's second-oldest profession. At first, people used a barter system for trade. Then, once currency was introduced in around 200 B.C., people started exchanging metal pieces having different values for buying and selling goods. However, only a small number and variety of goods were available, and they did not require any kind of aggressive selling. People simply bought things based on their needs. However, the Industrial Revolution at the turn of the 18th century changed things completely.

The period from the late 18th century to almost the end of the 19th century saw rapid social changes. Goods began to be mass-produced. More importantly, different companies started producing the same goods, thereby creating competition. Companies thus had a need to inform potential customers of how their product was better than that offered by the competition. And thus, salespersons were born!

The last century was dominated by two main sales techniques: *manipulative* or *barrier selling* and *relationship selling*. Manipulative selling emerged in the 1940s. In this approach, salespersons would ask a potential customer leading questions that always had a 'yes' answer. Instead of focusing on the product and its features, they used psychological techniques to either scare or coerce the customer into buying the product. Therefore, customers often ended up buying products that they did not really need. This approach thus gave salespersons a bad reputation. At the same time, as people gained access to more information through different media, they became more difficult to manipulate.

In 1936, Dale Carnegie published his seminal book called *How To Win Friends And Influence People*. This book changed the way in which salespersons looked at potential customers, and it ultimately gave rise to the concept of relationship selling. This approach emphasized the importance of building a rapport with customers and gaining their confidence before making a sale. The presumption was that once a potential customer liked and trusted the salesperson, they would buy repeatedly from them regardless of factors such as price and needs. The way social media is used today for selling shows that this approach remains popular and powerful.

During the early years of the Industrial Revolution, companies did not always *brand* their products. Therefore, *selling* was not a requirement. However, with the development of better roads and railways as well as faster vehicles, customers could easily acquire products from distant places. Companies now required methods for distinguishing their product from those of competitors, and this created the need for branding. The increase in branding over time led to the need for aggressive sales and salespersons. Salespersons had to convince customers that their company's product was superior to that provided by competitors.

Companies gradually started understanding how customers' behaviour patterns would impact their buying behaviours. They realized the need for individuals who could study markets and consumers. *Sales and marketing* professionals became an integral part of teams that would decide why, when, and how much of a product would be manufactured and where it would be sold. In time, their customer insights started playing an increasingly important role in the development of new products and promotional strategies.

Companies now started focusing on building customer and brand loyalty. Philip Kotler noted that the *'cost of attracting a new customer is estimated to be five times the cost of keeping a current customer happy'*. Brand loyalty emerged as the most important aspect of being profitable. Companies recognized the need for customers to have a relationship with the brand and for the brand to become personally relevant to them. With this shift in thinking, marketing became less about the company and more about the customer.

With the advent of the Internet, traditional methods of selling and marketing became obsolete. As customers became more aware and sophisticated, their demands changed. Nowadays, potential customers want bespoke solutions to address their specific needs. They compare companies in terms of the value addition they provide. Therefore, what works for a company today may become ineffective tomorrow. To be effective, you must be ready to constantly adapt your selling techniques in line with the new demands and technologies of the future.

Retail Selling

The main purpose of selling is to identify a problem the customer has, provide them with a solution, and explain how your solution is better than that offered by your competitors.

Retail selling involves directly selling a

product/service to an individual customer for their personal use. Companies need to do *market research* for this purpose. Furthermore, they can use various *channels* for selling, such as a brick-and-mortar store, online store, or mail-order selling. Salespersons should be mindful of the following in retail selling.

You will usually be limited to one product line, making it imperative for you to sell the product you have.

You should try to customize a product/service according to the client's requirements to maximise sales. For example, instead of selling a printer that can only print documents, try to sell one that scans, faxes, emails, and uploads documents to backup servers.

You must work hard to convince the client about the quality of your product or service so that they are willing to pay a premium for it.

Consultative Selling

The Internet gave clients much greater access to information and made them much more aware of the market. Salespersons thus had to switch from *manipulative selling* to a *needs-based approach*. Accordingly, they changed from pushy, aggressive individuals to consultants who provided guidance. Salesperson–client interactions have become much more collaborative, and the focal point of sales has changed from the product to the client's needs.

The cornerstone of consultative selling is to *know your clients and their needs*. You can then sell a tailored solution that delivers exactly what your client is looking for. This is a skill that requires constant practice to develop.

To be successful at consultative selling, you must be authentic and trustworthy. Also, you must develop a nuanced understanding of the client's needs and then try to fulfil these needs through a customized solution.

Watch out for these important points in consultative selling.

Know your client: Most salespersons consider themselves to be customer-focused, but very few of them truly are. In fact, McKinsey & Company found that around 60% of customers surveyed said that their salesperson was not aware of their needs. Therefore, you must examine your sales pitch thoroughly and determine whether the client is really at its centre.

Focus on your client: When making your pitch or telling your story, you must consider this question: is the central character your product/company or your client? If it is the former, you need to change your entire pitch. The hero of your story must always be the client, and your entire narrative should be aimed at convincing clients to change their buying decision and realize how their life is better with your solution.

Build rapport: It is crucial to be honest in consultative selling. Building rapport lies at the heart of making any human interaction, including selling, a success. You must remember what you know about your client, including their interests and their problems, and comment on it. Such interactions seemingly work simply because they cannot be scripted. Each client is unique and interesting, so you need to build a relationship that goes beyond making a sales pitch. At the same time, remember that there is a fine line beyond which you may come across as overfriendly or as a suck up, thus putting off the client.

Make recommendations: Always look for opportunities to recommend additional products or accessories based on what the client has already bought. For example, if the client has already decided on which IT server to buy, suggest add-ons such as an annual maintenance contract or consulting services. If you have built a good rapport with your client and are honest, you can upsell more easily without being pushy or forceful.

Question and probe: Think of your product/service as a jigsaw puzzle for which you have all the pieces.

However, *you* do not know what the finished picture should look like. Only the *customer* does. Your job is to put the pieces together and complete the picture by asking the client simple questions to build up to what they actually need. For example, if you are selling recovery software, ask the client about their backup processes and use their answers to formulate more leading questions. By listening carefully to the client's answers, you can pick up verbal and nonverbal cues to create a better understanding of the final picture, that is, the client's needs.

Know when to stop the pitch: The sales process is not a linear process. You must realize that no matter how much information you provide and benefits you offer or how well you know the client, at some point, your sales pitch must end. At the end, the client will choose you or your competitor. The client might even decide to not buy from anyone. In fact, studies show that 20%–60% of deals in the pipeline are lost to 'no decision' rather than to competitors. To make it easy for the client to choose your product, convince them of why it is the best for their needs.

Add value: In all likelihood, the product/service you offer is quite similar to that offered by your competitor's salesperson. So, instead of focusing on the features that are identical, focus on those that are different. You must define the value proposition very clearly and enable the client to see how your product's value addition is unique and essential.

Business ethics: All salespersons know the line '*He could sell ice to an Eskimo*'. This is usually considered a *compliment* of a salesperson's selling ability. But really, it highlights what a salesperson should *not do*. After all, why would an Eskimo need ice? An honest salesperson would not sell products/services that are not useful to the client. While such a sale may help the bottom line in the short term, it will do more harm than good in the long term. Clients will probably realize that they cannot trust you and will not return to you. Worse, they may spread word of your dishonesty.

Respect your client's research: Remember that most clients will come to you armed with all the information they can find about your product. Furthermore, clients usually meet several vendors, so they are probably well-informed about your competitors' products too. Therefore, you must be able to answer any and all your client's questions about your own product. At the same time, you must study competitors' products and then identify the unique benefits of your own product so that clients will not have the upper hand on you.

Go the extra mile: You must provide the client with the best after-sales service or follow through if they have not yet closed the deal. Also, show genuine interest in the client even if the sale does not go through as clients will remember such efforts.

Consultative selling sounds easy in principle. But in practice, it is a skill that needs to be perfected over time. You need to have razor-sharp focus throughout the entire selling process to show the client that you value them and their time. A misstep could easily turn into a missed opportunity.

ANATOMY OF A FULLSTACK SALESPERSON

What is a FullStack Salesperson?

A FullStack salesperson handles the entire sales process from prospecting to presenting to closing the deal. They control the sales process from start to finish. Thus, a FullStack salesperson can monitor developments, identify pain points, make necessary fixes and improvements, and ensure consistency. This is essential for delivering high-quality service to clients.

What Makes a Good FullStack Salesperson?

A company's revenue and overall growth will likely depend on your ability to woo and, ultimately, win clients. To make this happen, you must possess most, if not all, of the following traits and abilities.

Empathy: Being empathetic is an important part of being a good FullStack salesperson. You must listen to the client and try to understand what they are asking for by stepping into their shoes. Avoid judging the client or letting any ulterior motive guide your actions; at the same time, give clients the space to express their concerns. By doing so, you can better understand and interact with them.

Curiosity: A FullStack salesperson needs to be curious and completely knowledgeable about their product and their client. If you know all the relevant details of your product, you can answer any and all client queries. A plus would be to know all there is to know about your competitors' products, especially in relation to your own product. Finally, you must be aware of current market trends and clients' specific needs. For these purposes, use all means and tools at your disposal for market and product research.

Adaptability: A FullStack salesperson must mould the entire sales process around the client's needs and constraints. After all, *the customer is king*. Adaptability will enable you to respond to the client's changing needs and to be flexible in accommodating them. You must also learn to adapt your sales strategy based on the client's profile and behaviour. Remember that different clients may respond positively to different sales pitches; at the same time, the same client may respond differently on different days. Therefore, you must work as if *nothing is certain* and adapt yourself to the situation you face.

Passion: A FullStack salesperson must be a passionate cheerleader for their product and company. You must be passionate about not only meeting targets but also building long-lasting relationships and realizing career growth. You must aim to not simply make a sale but to make a change in your client's life. So, you need to be passionate about every part of the sales process and not just its closing. You need to believe in your product and sell it with conviction.

Ethics: Salespersons might think that ethics and being successful at sales do not always go hand-in-hand. However, if you value client relationships and want clients to keep coming back, it is critical to never intentionally misrepresent anything about your product/service or company. Clients may occasionally have some incorrect ideas about your products/services or may misunderstand things about your competitors or about the needs of their organizations. When these wrong notions work in your favour, it is very tempting to ignore them. However, to do so would mean that you are not acting with integrity. It is your responsibility to correct the client if you realize that they have significant misconceptions that could impact their buying decision. Being ethical also means that you should avoid overpromising and always remain aware of what can be delivered. Of course, this does not mean that you should under-promise and then over-deliver, as most clients will see through this immediately and lose trust in you. Ideally, be honest about your products/services, stick to what is deliverable, and let clients know that you will go the extra mile but within reasonable expectations. At the same time, always avoid unethical conduct such as speaking negatively about your competitors, bosses, company, or manufacturers.

Communication and presentation skills: You need excellent communication skills to make a successful sale. This includes being able to talk clearly and to listen with attention. If you use too much jargon or difficult concepts when talking, clients may not fully understand you. At the same time, if you are not a good listener, you may miss out on valuable and useful information provided by clients. You need to pick up the client's verbal cues and body language as, together, both reveal a lot of even if the client is not actually saying it. Also, be mindful of your own verbal and non-verbal cues, and always try to present the best possible version of yourself to the client.

Being organized: For a FullStack salesperson, being organized is closely related to how knowledgeable they are about their clients. If your client-related information is more organized, you will likely have more detailed and precise notes on the client's preferences and on products/services they have bought previously, problems that occurred, and open issues. This will make it easier for you to keep the client happy. If you have more data on customers and are better organized, you will likely gain their trust for satisfying their business needs.

Smart worker: FullStack salespersons must always work as if the sale does not end once the deal closes. You need to remain the client's go-to person for any issues that might arise as long as they are using your product/service. It is your responsibility to get these issues or complications resolved quickly and efficiently. Remember that you will be aided by your company's support team, including engineers, after-sales personnel, technical experts, and management, to deal with problems that cannot be resolved easily. So, be a team player and call upon these allies when needed instead of being a lone wolf and struggling alone. In other words, you must know exactly whom to turn to for help and when.

Self-motivation: A FullStack salesperson cannot afford to constantly look for direction from superiors and be needy. You will simply end up wasting everyone's time and energy instead of better spending it by being in the field, taking risks, and learning from mistakes. Of course, you should avail of support and guidance when necessary, but only as the last resort. If you take responsibility for the product/service you sell, managers will trust your decision-making safe in the knowledge that even mistakes will be corrected and, more importantly, will not be repeated.

Resilience: Resilience is the ability to pick yourself up after getting knocked off your feet, learn from your mistakes instead of repeating them, and reject rejection instead of becoming negative. FullStack salespersons will hear a 'no' more often than they hear a 'yes' from clients. You may unexpectedly lose deals that seemed certain to be won, and you may have a dozen losses for every win. Your success will ultimately be determined by your response to rejection. If you are resilient, you will think about what happened, think of ways in which you can meet a challenge differently, and find a way to win. Thus, you must respond positively during stressful or difficult situations. Furthermore, stand strong during adversity and actively shift your mindset to being more confident, adaptable, and capable.

Reputation is Everything!

Does the bad reputation of an individual salesperson really cost the company? Consider the example of musician Dave Carroll and his flight with United Airlines. He witnessed the crew manhandling his guitar and ultimately damaging it. However, when he complained to the airline, they refused to pay for the damage. So, Carroll did what he did best: he wrote a song about his experience, called '*United Breaks Guitars*'. This song became a huge hit and was watched by millions. Following the video's release, United Airlines' stock fell by 10%, causing losses worth $180 million!

The salesperson is the first point of contact for both the client and the company. If the first experience is less than favourable, conducting business becomes that much more difficult. The client could end up giving bad reviews for the company based on their experience with the salesperson. While it is difficult to estimate the actual cost of a bad online reputation, certain factsheets place the annual cost of unhappy customers at more than $500 billion. At the same time, completely satisfied customers have been shown to contribute 2.6 times more revenue than only somewhat satisfied customers. Here, it should be noted that acquiring a new customer typically costs 6–7 times more than simply retaining an existing one.

The story of Uber is another good example of how bad reputation can almost break a company. Uber and Travis Kalanick, its founder, have both become brands that are synonymous with innovation and disruption.

Kalanick was passionate, determined, and committed to do whatever was necessary to make Uber a success. He grew Uber to amazing heights, with its valuation reaching $70 billion at one point. But then came the stories of Uber's toxic work culture and gender discrimination. Around the same time, a video showing Travis arguing with an Uber driver went viral. Evidence surfaced proving that Kalanick had encouraged Uber to flout transportation and safety regulations and to capitalise on legal loopholes and grey areas to gain business advantages and push the line. Uber's investors decided that Kalanick's flaws and the bad reputation they gave the company far outweighed his strengths, so they ultimately asked him to step down.

As a salesperson, what lessons can you take home from these stories?

No matter how good you are at your job, sometimes, it takes just one catalyst to turn the tide against you.

Just because certain methods worked in the past, they are not going to be effective forever.

When you are on top, every move you make will be watched, scrutinised, and analysed.

The case of Samsung illustrates how unethical behaviour can lead to the downfall of even a corporate giant. Samsung accounts for one-fifth of South Korea's GDP, and it has long been known for its ethical practices. In early May 2014, Lee Kun-Hee, Samsung's charismatic second-generation leader, suffered a massive heart attack that forced him to withdraw from the business. Jay Lee, his only son, was suddenly forced to step into his father's shoes and carry the legacy forward. Jay Lee took his future ownership and control of Samsung for granted, but he did not have a long-term plan. To tighten his grip on the company, the younger Lee and his advisers decided to merge Cheil Industries with Samsung C&T. This would give Lee the control he needed to ensure his succession, because C&T owned a large block of shares in Samsung Electronics, the crown jewel in the Samsung empire. However, this deal eventually landed him behind bars because he used illegal means to get the merger approved by the Korean state pension fund, which was the majority shareholder in Samsung C&T.

All these examples show that even one instance of unethical behaviour can destroy decades of good reputation. At the same time, an ethical salesperson could potentially turn decades of bad reputation on its head and change a company's fortunes.

IDENTIFYING A TARGET MARKET

For a FullStack salesperson, a successful sale largely depends on accurately identifying prospects and clients. The target customer cannot be everyone in the given business area. Marketing a solution to everyone will simply be a waste of time and energy. The target market should ideally include only those customers who are good fits for your solution. For example, trying to sell a hamburger to a vegetarian is a waste of time, effort, and money. You must define the target market for your business. Market analysis is an effective approach for this purpose.

Conducting Market Analysis

You need to conduct a market analysis to accurately identify potential customers. By targeting such customers, you can reach the right audience and efficiently use your resources to impress and attract the customers. The basics of market analysis are as follows.

Who: First, you must identify your potential customers and collect all relevant details such as their age, gender, education levels, and occupation.

What: Ask your potential customers about what motivates them and what their interests, hobbies, and needs are. Accordingly, try to understand the types of solutions and features they would be interested in buying. You can do this by determining what problem your solution can solve for the customer.

When: You need to determine the time period when your customers are most likely to buy your solution. This could be a specific time like a day, week, or month. Alternatively, it could also be a frequency (e.g. in a subscription model). You need to have an idea of when your customers are most likely to view marketing materials. Also, remember to consider customers' budget cycles because these will determine their buying decisions. Finally, consider factors such as whether customers would be more receptive at certain times of day and what medium is most likely to catch their attention.

Where: You must know where your customers are located, including whether they are located in an industrial zone or a central business district (CBD). For example, a customer whose office is in a CBD will most likely be in a corporate headquarters in a department such as sales, HR, or accounting, and a customer whose office is in an industrial zone will likely be involved in production- or processing-related activities.

Why: You must determine why a potential customer buys from you. An important aspect in this regard is whether a customer is more focused on service excellence or price sensitivity. For example, some prospects are willing to pay a premium price if they are assured of quality services. Also, try to determine why customers prefer you over a competitor. To do this successfully, you could conduct competitor analyses.

How: You need to determine whether customers have an elaborate procurement process or whether decisions are taken by the top management. Also, determine whether purchasing processes involve tenders or a request for proposal (RFP). Once you identify a target market, remember that a segment is dynamic and not constant. Therefore, as business grows, remember to continually evaluate and widen your target market.

Identifying a Need for your Solution

You will always have a solution to sell, but the client will buy it only when there is a *need* for it. Knowing exactly what customers want to buy and when can mean the difference between success and failure. Surely, you must wish that clients would give a signal—preferably, a smoke signal, loud and clear—when they have a need for your solution!

Well, actually, they do. Some signals may be quite clear whereas others may be more subtle, but they are certainly there. You need to identify and understand the client's signals from their viewpoint and come up with an angle where you can pitch to them. Remember that signals can be about both internal and external factors. As long as you spot them, they can indicate that your client is open to new ideas and discussions about a solution because they have a *need*.

Internal Factors

RFP or tender: An RFP or tender is the clearest signal you can hope to receive from a company. It indicates that the client is exploring the market, and it will indicate in detail what solution the client is looking for. This is a good opportunity to remind the company that you exist, especially if they do not already know you, and to then put your best foot (i.e. your solution *and* a competitive price) forward.

A state of change: Companies that have gone through a merger, expansion, or consolidation; a management change; and recent attritions or hiring sprees are typically good targets for salespersons because they are likely open to change and hungry for improvement. This usually translates into a willingness to make investments. For example, they may be willing to re-examine existing systems and technology, and they may be on the lookout for solutions to improve efficiency or manage costs.

Pressure on profits: A company that is struggling to make profits or working with low margins may not seem the most likely target for your solution because they might just lack the budget for it. But perhaps, this is exactly the company you are looking for, especially if you have a solution that can help them turn things around.

External Factors

Government regulations: If government regulations are about to change or have changed, they often create an opportunity for solutions (including new ones) that will help clients adjust to the new normal. For example, the European Union's recent General Data Protection Regulation (GDPR) enabled IT companies and consultants to sell and upsell solutions to clients and to help them upgrade to new systems to ensure compliance with the new laws.

Market share: Consider one client who is losing market share to competition and another who is gaining market share over competition. Both clients could be in need of your solution: the first, to close the gap to competition and the second, to consolidate the advantage over competition and improve it further.

Market reputation: Companies can sometimes suffer setbacks, such as financial frauds or mismanagement of funds and environmental, health, or safety issues and the resulting lawsuits. These events can destroy a company's reputation and goodwill in the market. In such situations, they will likely need solutions that help them improve processes and increase oversight and compliance.

This, in turn, will help them get back into the good books of customers and regulators and thus rehabilitate themselves in the market.

Testing Your Solution

Before actively selling a solution, salespersons must determine whether their solution fits the market. A fit is essential for identifying the correct customers, understanding whether the solution satisfies their needs, and determining the customer's willingness to pay. The following factors play an important role in evaluating the solution-market fit.

Unique selling proposition (USP): The USP is a simple statement that describes what customers will get when they use a solution. Salespersons must remember that they are selling not just a solution but an experience.

Target buyer persona: Salespersons must create an imaginary customer and identify their problems and challenges to determine whether these can be solved through their solutions. For example, if the target customer is a family-owned business or a small and medium enterprise (SME) wanting to digitize its business and automate and modernize its processes, the salespersons must determine the customer's goals and anticipate potential challenges they will face so that they can understand whether their solution will help with the same. Salespersons must also anticipate customers' potential objections and reasons why they might prefer a competitor's solution.

Competitor research: Nowadays, potential customers likely search online for solutions that can solve their specific problems. Salespersons, too, must search online using the same terms customers are likely to use to find their solution. Tools such as Google Trends are helpful for checking whether a given solution fits in terms of current trends. Specifically, salespersons can identify whether a trend is rising or falling or whether it has plateaued.

Customer interviews: Customer interviews are very important because they serve both as research and as potential leads that could convert into sales. Before customer interviews, salespersons must prepare a detailed questionnaire with precise yet concise questions and make research calls to companies. Their questions should cover requirements, business needs, policies, current systems in place, and typical buying process. Their questions should also cover competitors' solutions and their advantages and disadvantages.

Company Mining

Company mining is nothing but a search for stakeholders and decision-makers. You will often wonder whether you are talking to the right person in the sales process. You may have identified the most promising customer and delivered the perfect pitch. However, if this person actually has zero buying power, you have wasted your time and energy. Therefore, before a sales pitch, spend as much time as necessary to ensure that you will pitch to the right person from the outset. This is where company mining comes into the picture.

Leveraging common connections: You can use networks like LinkedIn to find common connections at a targeted company. Such a connection could help in getting an introduction with a decision-maker at the company.

Mapping the organization: Various commercial tools, including LinkedIn Sales Navigator, as well as advanced searches can be used to map an organization, visit profiles, and identify likely decision-makers in a company.

Scrutinizing profiles: A close examination of profiles reveals two important types of information. The first is the length of service. For example, if a VP has only been at a company for two months but a Director has been there for three years, the Director likely has more influence and buying power. The second is the skills and endorsements; this can give a sense of who is qualified to make buying decisions.

Approaching the prospect: You can use either top-down or bottom-up approaches to reach a prospect. In a top-down approach, you start at the top of the hierarchy and contact someone in top management, such as a VP, to ask for a referral down to the right person. Of course, the work becomes a lot easier if this person is, in fact, the decision-maker! In a bottom-up approach, you start at the lower levels of an organization to try to reach someone who is higher up. This approach can be particularly effective with sales reps. If you can convince sales reps of how your solution will make their lives easier, they may be willing to go to their bosses on your behalf.

News and press releases: Examine industry- and company-specific news to understand what is happening on the client front. This may also give you an understanding of potential requirements. For example, if a company is known to be on the verge of buying out a competitor or starting a new business venture, they likely need services related to mergers and acquisitions (M&A), such as company information, macroeconomic data on other countries, and transaction advisory services.

Who is the Decision-maker?

Decision-makers' titles can vary greatly across organizations. In some cases, you may even need to make an educated guess based on company size to identify the decision-maker. For example, in a small company, the CEO or VP is usually the decision-maker, whereas in a large company, buying decisions are made by specialized roles such as the sales manager or business development manager.

Decision-makers and their titles also vary with the *type of organization*. Consider the different industry examples given below:

Financial: The financial industry might have people with different roles such as Risk Management, Analyst, General Manager, and Procurement Manager. You need to understand what functions these roles entail before deciding who you must pitch your solution to.

Government: If you are planning to sell a solution to the government, identifying who holds the decision-making power can be even more important but just as challenging. Usually, the government includes local, state, and central governments as well as their corresponding bureaucratic offices. Therefore, different layers of decision-makers can exist, such as contract agents and acquisition staff. You might even have to sell your solution to *all these layers* before they can make a buy decision. Therefore, prepare thoroughly to avoid wasting time and energy on the wrong person.

Technology: When selling to technology companies, again, you might have to pitch to all levels. Therefore, a bottom-up approach might be preferable. For example, you may have to convince the '*influencer*' who starts the buying process, the '*decision-maker*' who makes the final buy decision, and the '*user*' who is the first to use the solution. Procurement and Legal departments might also be involved.

Real Estate: Because real estate is usually an investment-heavy sector, most buy decisions are made by top management such as the CEO or VP. These are the people who you need to target.

Healthcare: In modern healthcare systems, multiple representatives make decisions about patient care and operations. Doctors, nurses, front-line, middle, and senior managers, and boards of directors all play key roles. Based on the solution, you need to determine who holds decision-making power. At the same time, even if the final decision is made by senior management or the board of directors, you might need to pitch to the doctors and nurses who are actually going to use the solution.

CREATING A MEMORABLE CUSTOMER BUYING EXPERIENCE

Imagine you are sitting in front of a tough prospect who has been particularly difficult to get a meeting with. You are fairly sure that your solution is the right one for the client and that it will help them greatly in meeting their business goals. You have run the numbers, projected benefits, and all possible objections, and there is really nothing that can stop the sale from going through. However, your customer—the one who was almost a sure thing—just said no!

All veteran salespersons will tell you that you must know when to *stop selling*. If you keep pitching while the prospect is already *giving you buying signals*, you may actually *lose the deal*.

This chapter will help you understand the factors you are dealing with, the people behind those factors and how to navigate through the maze in order to ensure your client has a memorable buying experience. The same will help ascertain the probability of the deal coming through.

Factors That Help Measure Buying Signals and Likelihood of a Sale

Buying signals are behavioural cues that indicate a prospect's or customer's readiness to buy. They can help make the sales process more efficient and result in higher yields. You must know how to read these buying signals so that you have the information you need to assess the pipeline for the given opportunity.

A salesperson's worst nightmare is to not know *why* a customer does or does not buy their solution. To understand this decision, you must understand the underlying factors or motivators. Knowing these will also help you draft intelligent proposals and business cases.

Company, Systems, and Individual (CSI) factors will help you greatly in better structuring your sales meetings. You should be able to assess the likelihood of a lead converting into an actual sale based on your solution being able to satisfy or improve the result for certain CSI factors. If your sale does not go through, all you need to do is check where your solution fell short of the CSI factors.

Company Factors

Company factors motivate a client to buy a new solution because they believe that it will enable them to improve their business by increasing profitability, efficiency, or hit ratio; introducing new or additional products/services; improving volume or quality of outputs; or managing risk better. Salespersons must understand and identify the company factor that is of prime importance, non-negotiable, and a must-have for the client. Consider the following examples:

Cloud-based services are popular nowadays because they make businesses more agile and more profitable by lowering in-house IT infrastructure costs and office space requirements.

Businesses tie-up with overseas companies because

this is an effective way to enter overseas markets and thus expand and grow.

Companies lease equipment like cranes and other construction technology to build taller buildings that increase revenues with only incremental increases in costs.

Systems Factors

Sometimes, a seemingly positive deal falls through simply because neither the client nor the salesperson brought up systems factors. Systems factors are often ignored or come up too late in sales talks, and both sides simply assume that they will work out!

Systems factors are critical in sales when your solution needs to fit in or be *compatible* with the client's ecosystem of existing applications. For example, you will not be able to push through a sale for MacOS-based software if your client's office uses only Windows-based systems. Similarly, your client will not buy a payment system which only supports a specific Bank's transactions when they prefer transactions using Visa and Mastercard.

You will not make a sale if your solution requires the client to completely overhaul their systems before it can be used. The business case will likely be very difficult, and the return on investment (ROI) will probably be poor. However, if your solution can be integrated with the client's existing systems, your business case will be more promising and favourable. Therefore, remember to always ask about the client's current systems and processes during a sales meeting, and enquire about the level of automation or manual work required to get the desired output.

Consider the example of a risk officer in a small regional bank in Southeast Asia who manually entered numbers from a PDF report into an Excel sheet for analysis. This process was long, arduous, and error-prone. In this case, the system factor is an Excel sheet, and if your solution can import data from a PDF into an Excel sheet quickly and without errors, the prospect will buy it. Now, imagine you dig a little deeper and find that once the analysis is done on the Excel sheet, it is then presented to the C-level in a PowerPoint format; this becomes another system factor to make note of.

Now, consider the example of a salesperson who approached a client to provide them with a regional travel management service. The solution proposed was a centralized travel management system for the client's offices in Asia. However, given the nature of the business, legacy systems, and established processes (e.g., for taxation), the client insisted on local currency invoicing and pricing for each office location. However, the salesperson's company could only provide invoices in USD from one central location. Obviously, the system factor was not met, and the sale did not go through. In this case, however, the salesperson could have advocated that their solution need not adapt to the client's existing systems. Instead, the client could consider a system upgrade, thereby also matching up with competitors; this could possibly result in a deal.

Individual Factors

A simple question lies at the core of individual factors: '*What's in it for me?*'. Individual factors are invisible and personal in nature, and they can have an impact on your sales process in mysterious ways. As a salesperson, you need to understand the personal ambitions and motivations of the people you are meeting. With a bit of attentive listening, you can determine individual factors through the questions your clients ask and how they approach your ideas and solutions.

Individual factors can include wanting to impress the senior management, promoting a solution that makes their work easier and faster, promoting the solution of a company where their spouse works, not signing a product deal that basically threatens their own job (e.g. via redundancy or irrelevance), being able to leave early and spend time with family, and fear of rapid change or of learning new technology. Once you can successfully gauge the factors motivating your client, you can use them in your favour. If your client favours another solution over yours because their family member works in the other vendor's company, then you must realize that the stakeholders need to be engaged directly and that you should not depend on this individual to take your business case forward. By contrast, if a client wants to promote your solution internally, provide them with all the support possible, including drafting their internal proposals, to help them shine in front of their management.

Identifying Stakeholders in Decision-Making

It is critical to identify key stakeholders in the decision-making process for the following reasons:

- Identifying key stakeholders in a decision-making process is very important for a sale to go through. Understanding the informal relationships that exist within a formal hierarchy will give you a roadmap of who you need to talk to.

- Identifying each stakeholder's role in the decision-making process will help you during the final rounds. For example, an executive's ability to *influence* a decision does not always guarantee that they will be involved in the *final* decision.

- Research shows that a typical complex B2B buying decision involves an average of at least 7 actively engaged stakeholders. So, if you have not identified this number of engaged stakeholders, you might be missing someone important!

- You must also look at the number of departments

a decision team includes. Typically, a decision team could include strategic, financial, operational, technical, and contractual departments. In rare cases, one person might represent more than one department. If you cannot identify the people representing a given department, you are unlikely to have a positive result.

Furthermore, stakeholders play different roles in the company, as listed below. Therefore, their needs and expectations in the decision-making process differ, and you must tailor your sales pitch to cater to each one.

User: The users are the ones who use your solution or experience your service first. They will likely use the solution every day. An effective solution can make their lives easier and get them interested in its functionalities and direct advantages. Conversely, a solution that is not user-friendly or intuitive will make their lives more difficult. For example, in current-generation technology, users demand cross-platform availability with desktop, laptop, and mobile versions for ease of use. However, if front-end users are unhappy with the offered functionality, they could raise issues with higher management and therefore negatively impact your efforts.

Manager: The manager's aim is generally to ensure that a solution will help the staff do their work more efficiently, as promised or expected.

Influencer: The influencer is an experienced person who helps influence the decision to choose one solution over another. They are usually a part of middle or senior management or ones who are well regarded within the company. They could also be external consultants who help in the decision-making process.

Decision-Maker: The decision-maker decides which solution to select once all options have been evaluated and all above-described individuals, namely, the user, the manager, and the influencer, have given their opinions. This person is usually responsible for an important business aspect such as the profit and loss of a department or business unit. The decision-maker's responsibility is to weigh the cost-to-benefit ratio and to determine whether a solution is economically feasible or viable with long-term effects and benefits. They also control the budget and are aware of budget allocations, and therefore, they are the ones who negotiate the price and other aspects of your proposal.

Signing Authority: The signing authority could be the same as the decision-maker or could even be a different person you do not know or have not met. This position is usually present in large corporations wherein the decision-maker only signs the internal documents and business cases for budget allocation but not the contract. A C-level person actually signs off on your contract.

How to Get the *MOST* out of Client Meetings

As a salesperson, have you come up with *guesstimates* (e.g. for numbers and time frames) that you thought were accurate, only for the deal to fall through later? How do you ensure that you have covered all your bases with a potential customer or deal? The checklist below will help you to gauge the likelihood of the deal succeeding and therefore accurately predict the sales forecast or pipeline. Remember to ask yourself these questions during an *appropriate stage* of the sales process.

M – Money

Does the client have *money* to spend on the solution? Are they aware that money needs to be spent first to later save money, make more money, make things better, or achieve other business goals?

Is *money* an issue? Is there a budget constraint?

To mitigate *money* issues for the client, is there a way

you could tweak your solution or something your company could do (e.g. offer the client a discount or part-payments/instalments)?

O – Options

What are the *options* available to your client (e.g. making a change vs. staying unchanged, other solutions)?

Which industry competitors are likely to be approached for a similar solution? Will your client choose the *option* to be proactive as a buyer or wait for others in the market to make the first move?

What financial and legal *options* for the client do you need to be aware of?

S – Solution

Do you have a viable *solution*?

Can other *solutions* be combined and packaged for the client?

Is the *solution* likely to minimize the client's problem? Does the client acknowledge this fact?

Does the client see the value of the *solution* in terms of what it promises to deliver?

Is your s*olution* likely to be relevant to the client in the coming years even with changes in regulations, taxation laws, government policies, international trade, etc.?

T – Time

What are your client's *time* frames from discussion to decision-making?

Are these *time* frames fixed?

What would help to bring forward or delay these *time* frames?

Stages of Selling & Buying Process

Time is a Relative Concept

Although *time* is the main factor in a sales process, you will realize that it is a *relative* concept based on whether you are the seller or buyer and how big the client's company is. Unless your client is a very small organization under the leadership of one person, a number of departments and an equal or larger number of people will be involved, and each department will have time factored in relatively. For example, clients might say that they will get back to you '*soon*'; although this may mean a month or a quarter for you as per your sales targets, it may mean six months for the client. Therefore, it is essential that you get your client to define timelines.

If you are sure that the proposed solution is viable, and your client sees the value in buying it, it may be a good idea to test the client's definition of time by suggesting actual dates and weeks in an estimated timeline and seeing if they agree. For instance, you could say '*Given the urgency of your problem, the fact that our solution helps you solve this problem, and the fact that you have the means to purchase it, I estimate we can iron out the contract T&Cs by next Thursday and have it signed by the following Monday. After that, I could have the internal processing of papers done by Wednesday and we could go live by next Friday. Does that timeline sound about right to you?*'

In reply, your client could either say 'yes' after giving it some thought or be completely shell-shocked if they are not ready for such speed. At this point, they will tell you how their internal processes work, thus giving you a much better estimate of the time involved in their decision-making and processing. Your prospect might reply with '*It takes my Legal team two weeks to get back on the most basic contracts and here we have several new terms to look at, so my estimate is they will take at least three weeks on this. In the meantime, I have to present this to the senior management (Board,*

CEO, CFO, etc.) after checking their schedule. They are most likely to be available only after (certain date). You might have to come back then for another presentation and recap to them. For now, I estimate this will be signed and processed in approximately three months from now. We can then expect to go live by the third or fourth month'.

While getting a client to define their timelines, a FullStack salesperson must be aware of their own internal department's timelines. If you assume your company will be fast in onboarding a new client and then realize that mobilizing your own team takes longer, it could lead to embarrassment and failure of commitments made to clients. Therefore, ensure that your own timelines are accurate and then get the client to explain theirs. Then, factor in these timelines and add one to two months to give an estimated date for closing the sale in the CRM sales pipeline. Even a million-dollar contract, although signed and agreed upon, may sometimes not go live for 2–3 months as the vendor will have to set things up, such as hiring and training new people, getting the software ready, and ensuring that testing is done.

Selling and Buying Stages

It is important to understand that selling and buying are both processes that move in stages. Knowing which stage you are at will help you engage with clients accordingly and predict the likelihood of a deal coming through in the sales pipeline.

Research Stage

As a salesperson, you must be aware of whether your client is evaluating solutions in the research stage or review stage. You must be able to determine what criteria are being used in each stage to filter vendors. This will be an excellent opportunity to add any missing criteria; this may include something your company can fulfil as a vendor and thereby seal the deal.

Consider a typical scenario, where a prospect calls

you to enquire about a certain solution. Salespersons live for an incoming sales query, and you are eager to tell the prospect all about the unique selling points of the solution and how it is going to benefit them. The prospect then tells you that they want to know only two things: the cost and whether the solution can extract data and reports into Excel sheets. Though unhappy to be cut short in the middle of your pitch, you tell the prospect the price and that data *cannot* be exported into an Excel sheet. The prospect thanks you and hangs up, and you have a feeling that you will never hear back from them again while wishing that exporting to an Excel sheet was a feature of your solution!

In the above case, your prospect is in the *research* stage. They are not looking to buy over a phone call. They are only filtering the vendors based on a preliminary idea of what they want. They would not have said 'yes' even to a vendor who quoted an agreeable price and could deliver the required features because they have a few more criteria to evaluate. Admittedly, this can be a very tricky situation because you have no idea that having answered some client questions over a quick phone call could mean being excluded from a later-stage RFP, bid, or procurement process.

A more effective way to handle this scenario would be to say, '*Sure, I can tell you the price, but it'll only be a ballpark figure or a wide range (e.g. $20000 to $50,000) because we are skipping the entire needs analysis process. With regard to exporting into an Excel sheet, we have upgraded from that function based on market feedback and new technology. Now, all Excel-related functions are performed on-screen in this software solution. It may be worthwhile for your company to change over to the latest technology used by your industry peers. However, if you still want this function, I can check with my product team whether previous or older versions of this solution with this function are available*'.

A FullStack salesperson would know that the probability of such sales coming through is quite low.

Therefore, you should forecast prospects in the research stage with longer timelines and lower probability of winning. Once your prospect has all the information they need from initial vendor responses, they will likely discuss and evaluate it with relevant people. If you are called back for meetings to be set up for product demonstration and presentations, things will become a little clearer, and this will complete the research stage. What happens in these meetings will determine the next steps and whether you move on to the *review* stage.

Review Stage
The review stage is divided into three sub-stages.

Stage 1: In this stage, you will be given the specifics of your client's requirements. These will include several criteria and a hint of their ideal setup for the use of the solution. Most criteria will have to match the functional capabilities of your solution. At the end of this stage, you must ensure that you have enough information to send the first draft of a summary document based on the SPEC (Solution, Problem, Effect, Cause) formula (discussed below).

Tip: Always figure out which criteria are the most crucial or are must-haves. That way, you know whether you stand a chance or whether you should conclude the meeting and walk away.

Stage 2: Assuming that stage 1 has gone well and the prospect considers your solution to be valid, the next review stage begins with the first draft of the SPEC document. At this stage, the prospect should ideally request either a *live demo*, a period of *trial access to the product* (if physical in nature), *a trial of service*, or *a benchmarking exercise* to decide on the quality of the output. This stage is the most crucial part of the process, and you should be able to get a time frame at this stage based on your industry standards. The information you are able to gather during stage 2 will build up to the next stage, namely, *proof of concept* (POC). It is essential that you get all the review criteria or measurements in place before commencing any trials or benchmarking. Otherwise, all your efforts may fail. You should be on the lookout for the following:

1. Actionable data points that the prospect wants to see.

2. Points that are to be measured or compared against the prospect's historic standards, industry standards, or any other acceptable market standards. For example, the prospect gets to see an average of *seven* more market queries per day through your product platform compared to only *three* on their existing platform. This represents a *more than 100% increase* in queries when using your platform solution.

3. Quality of output, as both you and the prospect need to be clear and in agreement on the parameters by which to judge the quality before starting the trial. However, this can be tricky, and you will need to ensure you have specifics on this. For instance, if you are in the financial services industry and your solutions work with market information, it may be easier to compare the reliability and accuracy of your solution based on other vendors or general market standards. If your solution allows your client to use the solution (for free or for a nominal fee), then the experience or result of such usage should be documented so that both you and the prospect can review it jointly later. This will ensure that ambiguous statements like '*the quality was not good enough*' will not be made as both of you are aware of the result generated.

4. The *time frame* of the trial of service or benchmarking should be just right to help the prospect experience the unique features and to

document feedback. The start of a trial of service should be announced to all the departments and people concerned with constant reminders, day counters, or weekly statistics of usage sent to all the people involved at the prospect's organization. This ensures engagement and enough data for stage 3.

Tip: Have the criteria written down on a '*Product Trial Evaluation Document*' and get the prospect to sign off and agree on it before commencing product trials or benchmarking. This document will be of critical importance during stage 3.

Example of *Product Trial Evaluation Document.*

What to Measure	How & When we Measure	Previous Average Result	Trial Result	Rating out of 10
Incoming marketing queries	Count queries through dedicated mailbox and phone queries daily	Three emails and/or one phone call daily	[enter result from trial]	[client's rating]
Financial market information update	Data points refreshed hourly	8 of 20 data points refreshed hourly	[enter result from trial]	
User experience and system response	Ease of use, product features and customisation	Restricted to using product features, customization only in display, and no download of data	[enter user's comments and experience from trial]	

Stage 3: Stage 3 is the POC stage (*proof of concept*). At this point, you have got the prospect to say 'yes' to a trial

of service. The trial started and ended on the decided dates and went well. Your prospect has experienced your solution. Now, the prospect will make the final decision. You cannot accurately predict the outcome of the deal unless you have strong hints that all is in your favour. You must document everything that has been discussed and done since the beginning, including the trial evaluation, in a POC document. Highlight the trial of service results as follows:

1. Begin with the initial parameters drawn out in the *Product Trial Evaluation Document*.
2. Mention the start and end dates of the trial.
3. Include the names of all people and departments involved in the *trial/benchmark exercise* from the prospect's organization. Mention the name of the project leader (if any).
4. Add the names of everyone (people and departments) from your side who participated in the project.
5. It would be worthwhile to start with a summary or objective of the trial evaluation project, including a background of why the trial evaluation was done, to give the reader some context.
6. To highlight your solution's unique features and utility, mention unique points or parameters drawn out for evaluation to create a galvanizing effect.
7. Present the trial results clearly and honestly, as shown above in the *trial evaluation document*.
8. If your prospect has provided you with a ratings table, ensure that you highlight good ratings for parameters which were crucial in the evaluation and would support the prospect's buying decision.
9. If any part of your solution failed to give the expected result, ensure that you mention this and the reasons behind it.

The trial evaluation process may reveal an entirely different issue from what was actually being evaluated. If you have any insights or solutions on such issues, describe them and possible solutions you can offer in a separate section. For example, you could be evaluating how certain data points can be imported using some function. Later, you may find that the prospect is manually copying these into another document and then writing a full report on the analysis. What if you could simply offer them a document writing software and template that reduces their labour by half? You could then potentially sell a new solution or module!

The final review stage should be followed immediately by a proposal.

Initial Proposal Drafting using SPEC Method

Presenting proposals in the Solution–Problem–Effect–Cause (SPEC) framework can help to logically present your business case. This will help your client see your reasoning behind the highlighted issues that exist in their organization.

S – Solution

When you are drafting a proposal, ensure that you speak from the client's viewpoint and avoid sales pitches. Explain how your solution is relevant to the client's problems in terms of business and application by using the Company–Systems–Individual (CSI) model. Furthermore, explain the results that can be expected from the solution and the pain points that will be reduced (and to what extent) or eliminated by your solution.

P – Problem

Describe all the problems or issues your prospect faces in descending order of intensity. Do not even mention your solution in this section. Be specific when you are describing the issues and mention what your client has told you, and do not assume problems that could arise.

For example, in a bank's credit department, problems could include a lack of verifiable customer data, multiple review steps before filing reports, and old data available for evaluations. The effect of these issues could include incomplete reports on a customer, in turn resulting in inaccurate assessments and longer processing times for loans, and assessments not based on latest information, thus potentially exposing the bank to credit risk if the customer has a questionable recent credit history. These problems could arise because the bank is unwilling to invest or simply has not yet invested in credible data sources or vendors, data is inaccurate and not auto-verifiable and thus requires a manual review, internal IT setup or data subscriptions are not advanced enough to give the latest information, or the bank is just unaware that such data can be obtained for process improvement.

The solutions to the above problems could be proof of verifiable data available for use, ease of access to such data, embedding such information into the bank's assessment process, and making data fluid enough to move across several steps and thus require no manual intervention.

E – Effect

The effect of both the problems and the solutions must be highlighted here. The effect of problems needs to be specific, such as time, cost, rate, efficiency, consumption, and waste. Similarly, the effect of the solution must be explained delicately, and you should not simply match a solution to a problem.

C – Cause

You must give the causes of or reasons why problems arise or exist. Possibilities include the nature of the company, internal company policies, management decisions, government regulations, regulatory implications, legal implications, compliance issues, general degradation, outdated technology, or geopolitical climate. While identifying the cause, ensure that you avoid putting the blame on or pointing fingers at anyone in the client's organization.

In summary, when you present the proposal, first mention the *causes*, discuss the *effects* they have on your client's business and the *problems* that have arisen as a result, and, finally, describe the *solution* to each problem and its effect (i.e. the outcome you are working toward). In other words, the FullStack salesperson may already have the solution in mind; however, to present this from a client's viewpoint, you need to go backward, starting with the C in SPEC.

IMPROVING THE CUSTOMER BUYING EXPERIENCE

The 30-second Elevator Pitch

What is an elevator pitch? Is it delivered only in an elevator? Definitely not! An elevator pitch is a brief introduction to your solution or project. As a FullStack salesperson, you should not confuse elevator pitches with sales pitches. A sales pitch is a formal presentation, whereas an elevator pitch is delivered briefly as a part of a casual conversation. Ideally, an elevator pitch should be short and should consist of three main parts:

Solves a problem: Why would the prospect buy your solution? You are not selling your solution but the benefit or impact it could have on the prospect's business. For example, if you are selling an inventory control system to help manufacturers keep track of their raw materials, instead of telling the customer, '*We sell inventory systems*', tell them, '*Companies hire us to streamline their inventory, thus saving a million dollars on average*'. By doing so, you are outlining a benefit that is relevant to the customer's business.

Provides an advantage: What makes your solution different from your competitor's solution? If there is no advantage, you are selling your industry and not your solution. There is no reason why a customer would buy from you. You must highlight a distinct and independently measurable advantage of your solution instead of giving unsubstantiated claims and opinions. The advantage should not be emotional as this might be irrelevant to the customer. For example, saying *'We are the best in the industry and have a world-class solution'* may make little difference to the customer. However, saying *'Our solution is patented to deliver materials the day they are needed'* gives the customer a reason to choose your solution over your competitor's solution.

Gets a meeting: The worst mistake you can make in an elevator pitch is trying to close the sale. What you are looking for at this point is a fact-finding meeting where you can determine the customer's needs and mutually decide whether you can meet them. An actual business meeting will have a lot more people involved and will involve actual decisions being made. In this scenario, saying *'Give me a call if you are interested'* is as ineffective as *'I can send you a price quote'*. In the first instance, you have not asked for a meeting, and in the second, you are in the danger of trying to close too soon. It would be better to say, *'Maybe we should run some numbers. What's your availability next week?'*

Here are a few pointers for delivering a great elevator pitch:

Keep your tone conversational: Try not to use too much corporate jargon or acronyms. Use simple language and words you are comfortable with. It would be useful to practice your elevator pitch in front of a mirror until it rolls off your tongue. For example, *'We help businesses keep track of their customer contacts'* sounds much more meaningful than *'We provide enterprise CRM solutions'*.

Motivate and inspire the client: When delivering an elevator pitch, more than your solution, you are selling yourself. You are simply introducing your solution, and this might eventually lead to a sales pitch. Therefore, smile, make eye contact, and be friendly!

Know everything possible about your solution: You must know the differentiators that set your solution apart from your competitor's solution and be ready to answer any query that your prospect has.

Tailor your pitch to the audience: The key challenges that an IT Director faces will differ from those a Finance Director faces. Similarly, the benefits the two see from a solution will differ. Therefore, it is important to tailor this part of your pitch to the *buyer persona* you are pitching to. Remember, one size does not fit all!

Mention your name, role, and company name in your elevator pitch.

Objection Handling

Every prospect you face will have some objections or reasons why they are hesitant to buy your solution. To be a successful FullStack salesperson, you must know how to discover and resolve these objections. Objection handling is what you do when a prospect expresses concern about the solution that you are selling, but you handle that concern in a way that allows the deal to go through. A customer may object to the price, product fit, or features or simply brush you off. How you handle this will decide whether the sale succeeds or fails.

Objection handling should never involve pressuring or arguing with a client to back down. This will only result in you losing their trust and destroying the rapport you have built with them. Try to help your client come to a favourable conclusion on their own by presenting all sides of an argument. You must also accept the fact that there will be many customers who, despite all your valid points, will fail to see your viewpoint and will not go through with a sale.

Why Is Objection Handling Important?

If you do not address sales objections at the outset, your customer's opinions will only get stronger. In this case, you will have to work much harder in the final stages to address these issues. It is far better to proactively identify objections at the start and try to address them by asking questions like *'Do you have any concerns about this product?'*, *'Are there any obstacles that will prevent you from buying this product?'*, or *'Do you have any concerns about the results you will see with this product?'*

Avoid reacting impulsively to a client's objections. Instead, listen attentively, validate their concern, ask qualifying questions, and respond in a thoughtful way. Give your customers time to talk about their concerns in detail, and then repeat them back to them in brief to see whether you have understood them well. Next, study these concerns in detail to determine their underlying reasons. Finally, offer a neutral recommendation to your client. At this point, your client should usually be willing to hear you out because you have actually listened to their concerns and explored their rationale rather than giving a knee-jerk response. In addition, if you keep track of the most common objections you receive, you can refine your responses and find solutions faster. If a particular objection comes up repeatedly, do not wait for your prospects to bring it up; instead, address it early and seek a solution.

Some examples of objections you will commonly face and ways in which you can tackle them are listed below.

'The price is too high' or *'We haven't allocated any budget this year'*.

Objections about price are the most common ones, even among prospects who have every intention of buying your solution. However, whenever you are addressing this issue, never focus on price as a selling point. Instead, always draw the focus back to the solution's value and benefit to the customer's business. You can point out how your solution can help the client increase their business and perhaps solve the cash crisis.

'We already have a contract with competitor X', 'I can get a cheaper version of your product from X', or 'I am happy with X'.

If your prospect is talking to you when they are already working with a competitor, this is actually good news. It means that they are looking for a change and have identified a solution, so half your work of convincing the prospect has already been done. Now, you can focus on explaining why your solution is the best fit for the prospect. If your prospect raises a contract-related objection, you will have to think creatively and figure out a way to offset the cost of breaking a contract or demonstrate an ROI that will compensate for that cost.

At the same time, if the prospect is happy with your competitor's solution or thinks that it is cheaper, you must first determine whether they are playing you against your competitor to drive up discounts. Nonetheless, you must also sell your solution's features and points of differentiation that make it superior. Therefore, emphasize the overall worth and value your solution will bring to the customer's business while playing down the cost.

'I have never heard about your product or company', 'Your product is not the right fit for us', 'I don't understand what your product can do for our company', or 'You don't understand my business'.

Objections like these are actually requests for information. This requires a quick summary of your value proposition instead of a sales pitch. To address these objections, as a FullStack salesperson, you must have thorough knowledge of your solution and of your customer's business. Assure the customer that you have experience of working with similar businesses and have solved similar problems. If your customer needs a highly technical explanation, you could bring along a subject matter expert (SME) to better explain the features. In this scenario, you need to be very specific in detailing how your solution will help the customer in solving specific problems and expanding their business.

'I am not authorized to sign off on this purchase', *'I can't sell this internally'*, or *'My CEO/senior management isn't convinced'*.

These are basically objections about authority or ability to buy. You might simply be pitching your solution to the wrong person, so all you need to do is find the right one. You might only need to ask your prospect for the name of the right person and get your call redirected to them. You could ask them about all the objections they anticipate and help them develop the business case for adopting your solution.

Thus, successful objection handling ultimately comes down to the following:

- Understanding your solution, your customers, and your marketplace thoroughly.
- Being aware that objections about cost are really about value for money.
- Convincing your customer that your solution's differentiators make it a better buy.
- Finding the right person to sell to.
- Remaining calm and never taking objections personally.

Objections are an inevitable part of sales. Customers may have some legitimate reasons for not buying; nonetheless, you can work around their reasons and convince them otherwise. Therefore, the next time you are practicing your sales pitch, practice your objection handling skills as well. Every time you successfully overcome an objection, make a note of what you did and talk with other salespeople about the responses that work for them. Finally, remember that a sales pitch might not convert into a deal even if you address all customer objections well.

When Do We Start Negotiating?

As a FullStack salesperson, you will negotiate often, so it is important for you to focus on what you negotiate on and when. First, when reaching new prospects, you will negotiate with gatekeepers for getting connected to the right people. Then, after the initial contact or cold call, you will negotiate on whether it is worth the prospect's time to have an initial meeting and if so, what should be on the agenda, who should attend the meeting, how much time should be set aside, what date and time to meet, etc. Later, you will negotiate on the prospect's must-haves from a solution; whether you should perform a serious evaluation of needs and examine possible solutions; and whether to perform a *trial of service* or *benchmarking* exercise. Later still, you will negotiate on the price, value, product features to use, access rights, legal terms, finance/payment terms, termination clauses, renewal of service terms, etc.

Knowing what the client is negotiating on should hint at the stage in which the sale is. Conversely, knowing the stage in which the sale is should help you understand whether you should negotiate and what points you should negotiate on.

Tip: Do not drop your prices at the very first instance of a price question. This usually happens during or after an initial meeting. For instance:

Buyer: '*So what would the service fees be?*'

Salesperson: '*It's $100, but I'll give you a special price of $80! That's a 20% discount!*'

This simply tells your prospect that you do not respect your own pricing schedule and that everything is easily negotiable!

Remember that the goal of a negotiation is to reach a mutual agreement with the prospect about the value of your solution. Also, do not negotiate before the prospect is sold, and do not revert to selling once negotiations have started.

We Love Storytelling

Throughout history, starting from the first cave drawings, telling stories has been a highly effective form of communication. The London School of Business noted that people can retain 65%–70% of information shared via a story versus only 5%–10% of information conveyed through statistics.

In sales, people are being bombarded with information, and this reduces their attention span. Successful storytelling can thus become one of the most critical selling skills. Sales stories have been shown to have a profound effect on our brains and our behaviour. Paul Zak, a neuroeconomics pioneer, found that highly engaging stories can elicit powerful empathic responses by triggering the release of oxytocin, the 'trust hormone'. This can help your prospect build trust in your brand or solution, and doing so should increase sales.

Here are a few ideas for how you can hone your storytelling skills:

Combine hard facts with the story to appeal to the prospect's logic and emotions: Because you have to sell a solution, you cannot just have a narrative. For example, if you are trying to sell a marketing automation software, you could tell the prospect, '*I understand how hard you have to work to manually comb through a database, send individual emails to clients, and not have them tracked, organized, and so on. Imagine a world where all this can be done through software, where once the software is set up, it can send auto-responder emails after a user fills out a form. The software can also track who* *came from which site and how long they stayed, and it will keep your database organized and compartmentalized so that you can share the right message with the right buyer at the right time'*.

Use metaphors in your sales stories: Our brains relate to metaphors in a way that helps us to actually experience a story. During a sales presentation, such stories enable the prospect's subconscious mind to truly understand the value addition of your solution. For example, listening to a PowerPoint presentation where you just read off the bullet points will activate the language processing parts of your prospect's brain. But they will not feel anything else! Instead, when your prospect listens to a story, they will actually live the story!

Relevance is the key: If your prospect cannot relate to your story and it has nothing that they care about, you are just wasting their time. You must ensure that you do your homework and make your story relevant to what your client is looking for, and then they will be hooked.

What are the Key Ingredients of a Great Story?

Every great story has a structure. An engaging story has a *hero* who encounters *obstacles* and emerges *victorious*. In a sales story, the hero has to be your prospect. On the road to improving their company's efficiency and expanding their business, your prospect faces problems every day. For instance, the payments processing system causes problems during purchase orders, the marketing process is inefficient, and too much time is spent manually researching prospects and their background. To solve such problems, your prospect buys and starts using your solution. Ultimately, the hero (i.e. prospect) emerges victorious (i.e. enjoys success), because your solution helps them overcome the obstacles (i.e. problems) they faced.

As a FullStack salesperson, you must use the power of stories to create an impact in your prospect's mind and pave the way to closing deals.

MEDIUM OF SELLING

Importance of a Script in Phone Selling

Most salespeople have varying opinions on whether a script works when selling or prospecting over the phone. Those who do not like scripts will give reasons like *'Using a script makes you sound like a telemarketer'*, *'You must go with the flow, as scripts make you sound artificial'*, and *'Prospects can tell when you are reading off a script, and it turns them off'*.

However, there are some compelling reasons for using a script when selling over the phone, as listed below:

A sales script helps you have a good beginning

During a sales pitch, you must take control of the conversation right at the beginning. Once you have steered the call in the direction you want it to go, your conversation becomes easier, and your prospect will go along with you to some extent. This is where a sales script will help you, as it will help you direct the conversation.

It creates an atmosphere of expectancy

You must have a strong script to make it work. Word choices are crucial when forming a script, and a well-written script can create an atmosphere of expectancy. The right words will put your prospect in the right frame of mind to listen to what you have to say and subsequently make a purchase.

A sales script helps you be in control

When you are just starting out in sales, there is every chance that you will get nervous and feel that you are in over your head. You could get bullied by the prospect who is on the other end of the line because you do not have much awareness of the power dynamics. You might not be able to control where the conversation is going and lose your train of thought. Having a script will help you get back on track, and you can refer to your script when you are not sure of what to say next.

It ensures that enough information is given

When you are doing a sales pitch over the phone, your prospect is usually pressed for time and would prefer to end the call. To keep their attention, your pitch has to be very efficient and should not lead to a lot of questions from the client. When you follow a script, you can avoid these by disclosing enough information, but not too much, because that would give your client the upper hand. Of course, you eventually need to give your client all the information about the solution, but not right at the outset.

A sales script can be used by your successor

The greatest advantage of using a script is that other people can use it as well. Assuming that you are an experienced salesperson and that you want to hand over the job of pitching sales over the phone to a newcomer, a script will help them learn and follow your process. This will ensure that they are able to duplicate your techniques and get results faster.

Importance of Well-Written Emails

The goal of your initial email is to open a dialogue and not necessarily to sell something. If you get a reply, you know that the prospect is at least interested in what you are offering. Once the dialogue has started, you can explain more, add value, and gradually move the sales process to the next level.

Here are a few things to keep in mind while writing an email:

Write a compelling and truthful subject line: For example, the subject line *'Branding: Learn Why the Future of your Company Depends Upon it'* telegraphs the entire content of the message and promises a valuable solution or outcome.

Deliver a clear message up front: Your prospect is busy and impatient and does not have time to understand what you are offering through a 'teaser'. Therefore, be direct and succinct and start with a clear statement of what you are offering.

Do not combine multiple messages or offerings in one email: Your prospects have short attention spans. They will probably read only one message and simply choose to ignore the rest. If you want to send out multiple email sales messages, either write a separate message for each solution or consider an email newsletter.

Tell your readers about the benefits clearly: Tell your prospect how your solution will benefit them rather than only telling them what you are offering. For example, the message *'Sign-up for the Personal Financial Advisory and you'll get powerful, objective, personalized advice each week by e-mail on how to invest your money to enable you to reach your personal financial goals'* conveys a complete and impactful meaning.

Give your readers something of value: Your email could provide a special offer, discount, or freebie as this may compensate for the time spent by the reader on opening your email and reading it.

Include a call to action: Once you have enticed your prospect to open your email and read it, tell them exactly what you want them to do. For example, you may invite them to sign up for your free newsletter, enter a raffle, or even buy your solution.

Etiquettes of selling over WhatsApp

WhatsApp's sheer extent of connectivity and speed make it ideal for businesses to sell their solution. However, there are potential pitfalls to using a WhatsApp group to sell.

Here are some tips to ensure that your business WhatsApp chats remain professional and keep work/life boundaries firmly in check:

Basic manners: In the same way that you ask a client whether it is okay to email or call, you must extend this basic courtesy when using WhatsApp. Some clients may not appreciate being contacted on WhatsApp for any reason. Furthermore, when starting a group, always make introductions if all members do not know each other, just as you would do in person. The same applies if you are added to a group; always introduce yourself so your contact number can be stored.

Group size: To ensure that everybody's opinion is heard, it is vital that the group size be manageable (e.g. 5–8 members). If you are replying to a specific statement or question within the group, use the 'Reply' function so that it is clear exactly who you are replying to. If you need to expand upon a point, send a direct message to the person rather than to everyone in the group to spare them details that they do not need.

Group name: Ensure that your group name clearly outlines what it is about and for. Once you have achieved your goals for creating the group, thank everyone for their participation and close the group. It is essential that you treat the group like a meeting.

Appropriate messages: A work-related group is not the right place to send jokes or memes. You may not know all members personally, and therefore, what you consider funny might be offensive or irritating to someone else. There is always a time and a place for everything, and a business group is not the place for humour.

Emojis: When responding to business-related questions, it is always best to refrain from using emojis. If you have to use emojis, use them sparingly. The discussion reflects on you personally even if you are not face-to-face with your client. Furthermore, avoid using colloquialisms or abbreviations as these may not be clear to or appreciated by everyone.

Participation: Ensure that you participate. While you do not have to respond constantly or immediately, avoid being that silent, creepy person who reads all messages but never responds.

Timing: Ensure that you send business-related messages during working hours. You might occasionally need to send an urgent message during non-work hours; this is fine as long as you do not do it frequently. Furthermore, avoid sending messages on weekends unless you know that all members are working as well. You might be a workaholic, but the others need not be.

Use discretion: Avoid expressing strong opinions on sensitive issues such as religion, politics, or personalities in a work-related group. Keep your personal views to yourself and do not let them spill over into a professional setting.

Remember that WhatsApp communications can be used as legal evidence because conversations can be downloaded as a transcript in a text file.

Face-to-Face Selling

Face-to-face selling remains critical even today although almost everything has turned digital. It still remains the most effective way to sell, build trust, and ensure long-term loyalty. In fact, Meeting Professionals International reported that 40% of prospective buyers became new customers through face-to-face meetings.

Personalised selling is also known to often lead to a

higher rate of referral. A client who is happy with your service is your best advertisement. They are usually willing to refer you to others if they are satisfied with your sales process, solution, and after-sales service.

Creating an emotional connect with your client, understanding what your client is trying to achieve, emphasizing your brand identity, having an effective game plan, knowing your solution inside out, being confident, and building trust are important points. Having said that, there are a *few more* areas you must be aware of:

Appearance: Dressing appropriately according to the occasion and your client gives an impression of professionalism and contributes to trustworthiness and respect. If you are dressed casually, it could indicate a casual approach to the prospect's needs.

Grooming: If you are well-groomed, you become more confident in your ability to swing the odds in your favour. Grooming includes both your wardrobe as well as personal hygiene. Be aware that a prospect notices all these aspects.

Attitude: Above all, wear a positive and confident attitude on your sleeve. Your smile must be warm and sincere and one that elicits trust.

Preparedness: The importance of being prepared for all eventualities during your meeting cannot be stressed enough. You must ensure that you have a written agenda, printouts of any information you plan to give out, USB with backup data, laptop connectors, cables, backup battery, etc.

Do's and Don'ts of a Sales Presentation

Sales presentations can often make or break a sale. When delivering a sales presentation, remember these do's and don'ts.

Do rehearse, rehearse, and, yes, rehearse your presentation. The best salespersons might rehearse even 10 times before the big day so that they can 'internalize the content' of their presentation. Sure, you can 'wing it', but that is a risk you would take only after you have delivered many, many live presentations to prospects and clients. If you cannot find someone in your team to rehearse with, just use your smartphone to video-record your rehearsal and analyse that!

Do tailor the presentation to your prospect. Your presentation must be customized to be relevant to your potential client. You must be able to clearly convey how each feature and benefit can be helpful to their unique situation. Use clear and creative visual aids to outline features and benefits.

Do stick to the 60% time rule. Ensure that your presentation takes no more than 60% of the allotted time. There is no point if your presentation is dragging on and the key decision-maker leaves because they have somewhere else to be! Be clear and concise with your information and eliminate anything that is not directly relevant to your message.

Do be passionate about what you are selling. Turn your nervous energy into enthusiasm! You must believe in what you are selling; otherwise, your client will not believe in your words. Aim to create a connection with everyone in the room during your presentation and showcase the value of your solution.

Do be yourself and let your personality shine through. It is okay to use scripts and prepared presentations, but deliver them in your own style instead of simply memorizing or reading them. Use relevant stories to grab the attention of your audience. Ensure that you come across as genuine and knowledgeable.

Don't focus only on the features and forget about the benefits. It is entirely possible that your prospects have already searched your website online and are familiar with the features of your solution. Therefore, what they need to understand from you are the benefits for their business if they make this investment.

Don't use technical jargon or industry buzzwords without qualifiers, or you may risk losing your audience. If you must use it to explain your solution, ensure that your audience understands what you are talking about, as this will also give them confidence in your knowledge and abilities.

Don't forget about your speaking style and body language. Avoid speaking too fast, modulate your voice, and do not use too many fillers like *'you know'*, *'umm'*, and *'well'*. This can distract your audience and indicate a lack of confidence. Body language includes your facial expressions (including smiling), eye contact, body posture, and gestures as well as your attire. Good body language can reinforce your presentation, whereas poor body language can result in you losing the audience. Again, this should be easy to refine if you are rehearsing regularly.

SALES TEAM MANAGEMENT

Teams typically comprise multiple sales managers who all sell the same solution in the same territory. As a result, competition within the team can be fierce, and it is often a case of survival of the fittest.

To manage sales teams effectively, for example, in a B2B operation, the market can be split among team members in the following ways:

- Customer location: e.g. North, South, East, and West.
- Alphabetic groups: e.g. company names starting with A–F are assigned to Alice, those with G–L are assigned to Bob, and so on.
- Round-robin: e.g. the first company is assigned to Alice, the second one is assigned to Bob, the third one is assigned to Charles, the fourth one is again assigned to Alice, and so on.

Systematic Approach to Markets

A systematic way to approach the market does not necessarily slow the pace or complicate matters excessively. In fact, if implemented well, a systematic approach can enable you to cover the market effectively and deliver good results. Here are some ways in which to systemically approach markets:

Industry wise: You can categorize your prospects into their relevant industries to better judge the size of the potential market. Also, when initiating contact with a prospect, try to speak in the language relevant to their given industry. This will help in gauging common business issues that need to be discussed as well as typical objections that will need to be handled. In this regard, if your solution is already very popular with clients from a certain industry, it will be easier to sell its value proposition to other industry players. By contrast, if your solution presently has very few takers in an industry, you should exercise some flexibility in making changes (e.g. to price or contract terms) or enhancing your solution based on the gathered intelligence and feedback. You could hire industry specialists in the sales team to facilitate such efforts.

Peers of existing top accounts: Study your top clients and then identify their peers not only in the same industry but also with similar business activities, market capitalization, or operating revenue. This is because other prospects in the peer group will likely have similar needs and business issues as your top clients. Therefore, the SPEC will be similar and so will the value proposition of your proposed solution.

Quick wins: Aim to get some quick wins early in the selling cycle. While you can pin your hopes on the decision for the big quote you have sent, you could also just get going with that initial sale so that the prospect can start experiencing your solutions. A small but quick win early in the selling cycle will make it a lot easier to continue and broaden the conversation with your prospect. This, in turn, could even result in a big upsell later.

Good mix of large and small companies:

Salespersons often aim only for the big accounts. However, big accounts also involve a larger number of people in the decision-making process, and therefore, the sales cycle can be much longer. A smart FullStack salesperson will keep a balanced mix of big and mid-size deals in their sales pipeline. This increases the likelihood of keeping the numbers rolling in every month. The big wins that you score every few months will just be the icing on the cake!

Standard Operating Procedures

Having standard operating procedures (SOPs) in place will help sales teams to run on autopilot with minimum fuss and minimum management intervention. They will also ensure that sales activities are organized and, as a result, effective.

Unfortunately, many sales teams simply do not have established SOPs. Others have SOPs that are neglected. In both cases, the outcome will likely be sub-optimal. Team members will lack direction if they know their SOPs only as those files on the shared network folder that someone once said were important. Remember that team work is not just the thing that you do and discuss at the annual sales training sessions!

Ultimately, the effectiveness of SOPs depends on how well they have been implemented and enforced by sales team leaders and how well everyone in the sales team understands them. Here are some examples of SOPs that you could implement within your team:

- Logical (or systematic) processes for lead distribution within the team
- Processes for engaging prospects, including first contact, customised presentations for prospect meetings, etc.
- Rules for creating opportunity, for example, no opportunity created without meeting a prospect

- Logging all communications into the CRM and tagging them to relevant leads or accounts
- Standard templates for quotations, proposals, and contracts that have been reviewed by team leaders and the product team before sending to a prospect or client
- Recycling leads with more than 3 months of inactivity by assigning to another team member

While SOPs certainly benefit everyone, too many of them for every step of the sales process can greatly harm the speed of execution of sales activities. So, it is crucial to strike a good balance. Your SOPs need to be light and manageable such that they act as a *roadway*, and not a *roadblock*, to closing a sale.

Motivation Techniques

Motivation can be extrinsic or intrinsic in nature. For example, a great sales manager who leads by example, who acts as the cheerleader, and who has the power to inspire their team to *want* to reach their goals can serve as an *extrinsic* motivator. At the same time, your *desire* to follow the leader in achieving or even exceeding your goals can serve as an *intrinsic* motivator. Of course, whether you are motivated by extrinsic or intrinsic factors, remember to not overextend yourself and get burnt out!

Sales managers should employ a combination of the following motivation techniques:

Empower: When you see team members struggling to meet their goals, your first instinct might be to jump in and show them how to do it. But it would really be more effective to work with them so that they can come up with a plan themselves. You need to have a gut feeling for when to play the role of active problem solver and when to allow team members to figure out things on their own. If you let team members know that you are confident in their capabilities, you empower them to find a solution. At the same time, let them know that you are there in case they need your help.

Course correction: Although it may seem that avoiding confrontations with your team members at all costs is a good idea, studies show that confrontations can play a valuable role in motivating people. If you see a team member getting demotivated or, worse, burning out because they do not know what they are doing wrong, confront them. Here, it would be counterproductive to be aggressive or to yell or punish them. Instead, correct the course by confronting them, addressing the problem, and better understanding why they are struggling. Although it may strike you as being unlikely, your team members will thank you for it!

Be an example: You may have risen to the position of sales manager based on your reputation as a top-notch salesperson or your leadership or managerial skills. Whatever it may be, never underestimate the power of leading by example. Reset your attitude every day to a positive one and do your work ethically irrespective of how good or bad the previous day was. Also, join the front lines once in a while, pick up the phone, speak to a prospect, and close the sale: show your team what being a FullStack salesperson is all about.

Set goals: The goals you set for your team members must be reachable, but not easily. The goals could be monthly, weekly, or even daily. Make sure you discuss each team member's goals with them in a face-to-face. If they feel that they have a say in their target numbers, they will be more motivated to achieve them. Then, be proactive and flexible when evaluating their progress. Give your team the flexibility to come up with out-of-the-box ideas, creative selling angles, etc., and let them be as proactive as they can.

Build trust: Treat your employees with respect, gain

their trust, and establish a healthy working relationship, and you will find that they are less likely to slack off. An effective way to achieve this end is to make all processes transparent and to give your team access to data such as statistics, analytics, and metrics.

Reward system: Gamification has emerged as a popular motivational technique in recent years. It provides some friendly competition and builds morale. The marketing intelligence company Aberdeen reported that *when gamification is used, 85% of salespersons attained their quotas and 51% of new hires achieved their numbers in their first year.* So, come up with the right gamification for your team based on their preferences. For example, you could set up a digitized scoreboard and assign different points for a completed sale, a new lead, etc. Let all team members keep track of the scores, and watch as they compete and strive for better results! This could also lead to bonuses, team outings or dinners, or other monetary benefits. You could even have your CEO call your team or an individual member if they have delivered spectacular results. *Rewards could also be for intangibles* such as best attitude, best on-time rep, and best idea during meetings.

Communicate: Never underestimate the value of communication, whether through stand-ups or regular meetings. Talk to your team to discuss problems they may be facing or to reenergize them when needed. Also, provide timely feedback on the team's performance. If your words come a month after a target is achieved or exceeded, it loses value!

SALES ANECDOTES

Murphy's Law states that '*Anything that can go wrong will go wrong*'. This statement is particularly true when it comes to sales pitches. As a FullStack salesperson, you will often have to think on your feet. Irrespective of how well prepared you are for your pitch or your presentation, strange and unexpected things will find a way of happening to you!

As demonstrated by the anecdotes below, in such situations, one's presence of mind and ability to think out of the box can turn the tide.

'*Making Room for a Demo*'

Harold's potential client was a major architect and design firm that was playing hard to get. They had cancelled two meetings hours before the scheduled time with some lame excuses.

During his third attempt, Harold had copied a higher-up in the email, so he was pretty confident that this meeting would take place. He was thoroughly prepared with hand-outs, sample reports, company brochures, and client testimonials. Furthermore, his colleague had a very concise and effective demo ready to present. They were all set with their laptops and data dongles, as he did not trust the prospects would allow access to the guest Wi-Fi in time.

Based on his earlier experience of having meetings cancelled at the eleventh hour, Harold had a feeling that something was about to go wrong! Therefore, instead of waiting to be called and informed that the meeting has been cancelled yet again, he decided to call the client's coordinator and reconfirm the setup. As five attendees were expected, he had asked for a meeting room with a projector. Harold told her, '*As we are meeting at around 4 PM, maybe I could take everyone's order and swing by the coffee shop on my way to your office*'. The lady happily gave him the coffee orders and then added, '*Oh, by the way, we forgot to book the meeting room with the projector. We can meet at the reception lobby area. Hope that's okay?*'

Of course, that was not okay! This was not a get-to-know-me-over-coffee meeting! A projector and a screen were essential for the demo. With barely two hours to go, Harold figured the only solution was to take along a projector and screen. But, as luck would have it, the only working projector his office had was already in use at an ongoing exhibition!

Harold reckoned it was time to improvise. He needed a screen facing the client, and it could not be the laptop screen as it was too small for a demo. So, he grabbed two 21" monitors from his office and proceeded to the meeting. He set up the screens on a small coffee table in the reception area, but this meant that his colleague would have to keep the laptop on her lap owing to a lack of table space. Nevertheless, he figured this setup was good enough and decided to begin the meeting.

The meeting went unexpectedly well, and the client was very impressed with Harold for bringing the screens. They were very engaged with the demo and, needless to say, Harold signed the contract within a few weeks of that meeting!

The Day We Started on the Last Page

A couple of years ago, Anisha's company was invited to present their solution at the annual convention of a consortium of management universities. The convention was usually attended by B-schools and University decision-makers who had authority over budgets (e.g. administration heads and chief librarians). The format of the convention was such that the University officials would attend vendor presentations, throw questions at presenters, and later jointly decide on a singular vendor (of each category) for the consortium.

Various vendors wished to do business with the consortium, ranging from furniture makers of student desks to water filtration providers, to distributors of cafeteria spoons and coffee cups, to vendors who specialised in IT servers and computer accessories. Also, there was Anisha's company, a global data provider for empirical research studies.

It was well known that the consortium members would use every pressure tactic in the book to get historically low prices from vendors. In fact, legend had it that the vendors hated this event but needed the business, so they would give rock-bottom prices at the first hint of negotiations. Therefore, most presentations were centred around price rather than product or value and took barely 15–20 minutes to complete.

Anisha's company provided a premium-quality data service, something that A-list universities worldwide paid top dollar for. Her presentation was geared toward showcasing her company's global university clients to gain the confidence of the audience, demonstrating the data services they were paying for to justify the price and quality of product, and finally proposing a pricing structure to the consortium. She had rehearsed her presentation thoroughly to last 25 minutes with enough time for questions and discussions.

Anisha started the presentation by distributing handouts; she introduced herself and was on page 3, which showcased the list of global university clients. One gentleman chose this moment to blurt out, *'It's great that these big universities are your clients, but as we are in Asia, what are your product prices for the local market?'*

That question echoed through the auditorium, and a few seconds later came in a joint chorus from the others: *'Just tell us what it costs!'* So, Anisha, very calmly, asked them to turn to page 21, the *last* page of the handout, for the prices. She explained, *'As you can see, we are offering the package needed for research studies at $50,000 per university, per annum, for 25 users if signed today as a three-year contract'*.

There was complete silence for a few moments. Then, the rejoinder from the gentleman who interrupted her earlier: *'That's a lot of money! What's so great about this data service that your company charges so high when others charge just 20% of that?'* Anisha replied softly, *'For that, Sir, we will need to turn back to page 3, and I'll continue with my presentation'*.

As expected, Anisha did not sign-up any university that day at the convention. However, around six months later, three participating universities followed up and signed the contract… *at full price.*

CONCLUSION

A good sales technique has always involved being able to read the client accurately. Initially, the more aggressive the salesperson, the better they were considered. However, more recently, actively engaging clients has proved to be more effective. *Customer loyalty* is the buzzword that predicts how well your organisation will grow, because it has been found that retaining a client costs less than acquiring a new one.

Today, a *FullStack salesperson* controls the entire sales process from prospecting to closing the deal to after-sales service. Irrespective of what your solution is and who your clients are, qualities like empathy, adaptability, passion, ethics, motivation, and good communication skills are a must-have. A critical part of being an effective FullStack salesperson is to correctly identify your target clients and ensure that you are speaking to the right decision-maker. Once this is done, it is all about creating that unique and memorable *customer buying experience (CBE)* that will keep clients coming back for more and even bringing some referrals!

An effective method to win a client is to tell a *good story* in which they are the hero who faces numerous obstacles at first before finally emerging victorious by using your solution. Just as important are a detailed and visually creative sales presentation as well as the ability to anticipate and handle all objections the client may raise. During the sales process, remember to ask yourself the *M (money), O (options), S (solution), and T (time) questions.* Also, acquaint yourself thoroughly with the different buying and selling stages and then draft your initial proposal using the *SPEC (solution, problem, effect, and cause) method.*

Nowadays, the different modes of selling include phone, email, and WhatsApp. Despite all this modern technology, face-to-face selling remains the most effective and popular method of selling. Creating an emotional connection with your client is vital to sell, build trust, and ensure long-term loyalty. You must strictly adhere to the finer points of etiquette when using any of these selling modes. Also, the importance of appearance, personal grooming, and a positive attitude cannot be emphasized enough.

Whether you are a FullStack salesperson or a sales team manager, having *standard operating procedures (SOPs)* in place is always a good idea. As a manager, you need to be a great motivator, and be sure to get back into the field occasionally. You must also have a systematic market approach with a good mix of big and small clients from different verticals. This will guarantee that your sales pipeline keeps flowing and does not become stagnant.

This handbook is aimed at equipping you with the skills to become the best FullStack salesperson you can be. Whether you are a sales newbie or an experienced one, the information and techniques described herein should help you face the different challenges you will encounter during the sales process. There is a brave new world out there, and hopefully, this handbook will serve as an able guide on your journey as a FullStack salesperson.

ABOUT THE AUTHORS

Archan Bahulekar

Archan has been an ad writer, movie critic, and a freelance journalist.

He's spent the last decade leading sales teams across Southeast Asia, crafting customized solutions in credit control, compliance, transfer pricing, risk management and recently, online payments and FinTech.

In his spare time, he's either trying his hand at free verse poetry or rehearsing for the next lip sync showdown!

Robin Lee

Robin's background in crafting Xperiences includes stints in Silicon Valley and Wall Street as well as in the Legal/Compliance, educational technology (EdTech), regulatory technology (RegTech), insurance technology (InsurTech), and FinTech areas.

He has also been a songwriter, actor, director, educator, and choreographer.

We'd love to hear your feedback and comments on the book at fullstacksalesperson@gmail.com

For enquiries on sales training for your teams, contact the authors at hello@xperientia.io

Or contact the authors through the links below

Archan Bahulekar

Robin Lee

Printed in Great Britain
by Amazon